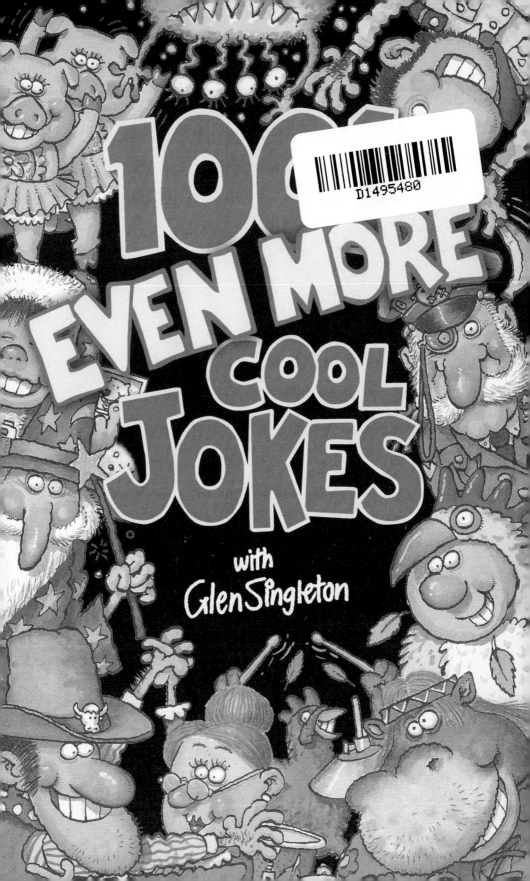

1001 EVEN MORE COOL JOKES

with
Glen Singleton

Cover Design: Ivan Finnegan
Cover Illustration & Illustrations: Glen Singleton
Jokes Collection: Nicolas Brasch
Typesetting: Midland Typesetters, Maryborough, VIC, Australia

1001 Even More Cool Jokes
Published in 2003 by Hinkler Books Pty Ltd
17–23 Redwood Drive
Dingley VIC 3172 Australia
www.hinklerbooks.com

ISBN: 1 8651 5868 2
Printed and bound in Australia

CONTENTS

Animals 4

Dinosaurs 44

Miscellaneous 48

Monsters, Witches,
Ghosts and Vampires 75

Doctor, Doctor 98

Food Glorious Food 107

Gross Out 117

Silly Inventions 126

Knock Knock 128

Riddles and Teasers 152

What do you call ... 158

Silly Book Titles 160

Classroom Capers 163

Making Music 168

Crossbreeds 172

Changing Light Bulbs 181

What a Wally 191

Insults 202

Animals

1   **H**ow do you get an elephant into a car?
Open the door.

2   **H**ow does the elephant get out of the car?
The same way it got in.

3   **H**ow do you know when there is an elephant in the oven?
You can't close the door.

4 **H**ow do you know when an elephant has been using your phone?

You've been charged for trunk calls.

5 **H**ow do you know peanuts are fattening?

Have you ever seen a skinny elephant?

6 **H**ow do you know when there is an elephant in the fridge?

There are footprints in the butter.

7 **W**hat did the mouse say to the elephant?

Squeak.

8 **D**id you hear about the elephant who drank a bottle of rum?

He got trunk.

9 **W**hat do you call an elephant that flies straight up?

An elecopter.

10 **W**hat do you call an elephant that flies?

A jumbo jet.

11 **W**hat do you call the red stuff between an elephant's toes?

A slow hunter.

12 **W**hat do you give an elephant with diarrhoea?

Plenty of room.

13 **W**hat's big, grey and sings jazz?

Elephantz Gerald.

14 **W**hat's big, grey and wears glass slippers?

Cinderelephant.

15 **W**here do elephants go on holidays?

Tuscany.

16 **W**hy are elephants big and grey?

Because if they were small and purple they would be grapes.

17 **W**hy do elephants have Big Ears?

Because Noddy wouldn't pay the ransom.

18 **W**hy do elephants have trunks?

Because they can't fit everything into a handbag.

19 **W**hy do elephants wear sneakers?

So they can sneak up on mice.

20 **W**hy was the elephant standing on the marshmallow?

He didn't want to fall in the hot chocolate.

21 **'A** bee just stung me on the arm.'

'Which one?'

'I don't know. They all look alike to me.'

22 **'D**oes your dog bite?'

'No.'

'Oww. I thought you said your dog doesn't bite.'

'That's not my dog.'

23 Customer: *'Have you got any dogs going cheap?'*
Pet Shop Owner: 'No,
I'm afraid they all go woof.'

24 'I play Scrabble with my pet dog every night.'
'He must be clever.'
'I don't know about that. I usually beat him.'

25 'I've lost my dog.'
'Put an ad in the paper.'
'Don't be silly. He can't read.'

26 What's the difference between a dark sky and an injured lion.
One pours with rain, the other roars with pain.

27 A pig walks into a bar and asks for a beer.
Bartender: *'That'll be $5. And by the way, it's nice to see you. We don't get many pigs in here.'*
Pig: *'At $5 a beer, I'm not surprised.'*

28 **A** grizzly bear walks into a bar and says to the bartender, 'I'll have a gin .... and tonic.'

Bartender: *'What's with the big pause?'*

Bear: *'I don't know. My father had them, too.'*

29 **C**ow 1: 'Are you concerned about catching mad cow disease.'

Cow 2: *'Not at all. I'm a sheep.'*

30 **C**ustomer: 'How much for the duck?'

Pet shop owner: '$20.'

Customer: *'I only have $15. Can you send me the bill?'*

Pet shop owner: *'No, you'll have to take the whole duck.'*

31 **D**id you hear about the duck who bought some lipstick?

She asked the chemist to put it on her bill.

32 **D**id you hear
about the duck
decorator?

*He papered over
the quacks.*

33 **D**id you hear
about the naughty
chicken?

*It was eggspelled
from school.*

34 **D**id you hear
about the
performer who
specialised in
bird
impressions?

He ate worms.

35 **D**id you hear
about the
cannibal lioness?

She swallowed her pride.

36 **D**id you hear about the acrobatic snake?
He was in Monty Python's Flying Circus.

37 **H**ow did the frog die?
It Kermit-ted suicide.

38 **H**ow do cows count?
They use a cowculator.

39 **H**ow do hens dance?
Chick to chick.

40 **H**ow do pigs get clean.
They go to the hogwash.

41 **H**ow do you know when a spider is cool?
It has its own Website.

42 **H**ow do you know when it's raining cats and dogs?
You step into a poodle.

43 **H**ow do sheep get clean?

They have a baaaaath.

44 **H**ow do you make a milkshake?

Give a cow a pogo stick.

45 **H**ow do you make a slow racehorse fast?

Put it on a diet.

46 **H**ow do you milk a mouse?

You can't. The bucket won't fit under it.

47 **H**ow do you stop a dog doing his business in the hall?

Put him outside.

48 **H**ow does a jellyfish race start?

Get set.

49 **S**heep 1: 'Baa.'
Sheep 2: '*I knew you were going to say that.*'

50 **W**hat are teenage giraffes told when they go on their first date?

No necking.

51 **W**hat did the 100 kilo parrot say?

'*Polly want a cracker, NOW!*'

52 **W**hat did the boa constrictor say to its victim?

'*I've got a crush on you.*'

53 **W**hat did the bull say to the cow?

'I'll love you for heifer and heifer.'

54 **W**hat did the cat say when it lost all its money?

'I'm paw.'

55 **W**hat did the fish say when he swam into the wall?

'Dam.'

56 **W**hat did the giraffe say when a car load of tourists drove past?

'It's terrible the way they're caged up.'

57 **W**hat did the lion say when a car load of tourists drove past?

'Meals on wheels.'

58 **W**hat do cats eat as a special treat?

Mice creams.

59 **W**hat disease do you have if you're allergic to horses?

Bronco-itis.

60 **W**hat do bees do with their honey?
They cell it.

61 **W**hat do bees use to communicate with each other?
Their cell phone.

62 **W**hat do cows listen to?
Moosic.

63 **W**hat do glow-worms drink?
Light beer.

64 **W**hat do you call a baby whale that never stops crying?
A little blubber.

65 **W**hat do you call a bee than buzzes quietly?
A mumble bee.

66 **W**hat do you call a camel with no humps?
A horse.

67 **W**hat do you call a cat who lives in a hospital?
A first aid kit.

68 **W**hat do you call a Chinese cat that spies through windows?
A Peking tom.

69 **W**hat do you call a cow that eats grass?
A lawn mooer.

70 **W**hat do you call a cow that lives at the North Pole?
An eskimoo.

71 **W**hat do you call a deer with only one eye?

No idea.

72 **W**hat do you call a deer with no legs and only one eye?

Still no idea.

73 **W**hat do you call a fish with no eyes?

Fsh.

74 **W**hat do you call a hippo that believes in peace, love and understanding?

A hippie-potamus.

75 **W**hat do you call a messy cat?

Kitty litter.

76 **W**hat do you call a mosquito that prefers walking to flying?

An itch-hiker.

77 **W**hat do you call a pig that does karate?

Pork chop.

78 **W**hat do you call a pig who enjoys jumping from a great height?

A stydiver.

79 **W**hat do you call a pig with no clothes on?

Streaky bacon.

80 **W**hat do you call a Russian fish?

A Tsardine.

81 **W**hat do you call a
well-behaved
goose?

A propaganda.

82 **W**hat do you call
a young goat who
visits a psychiatrist?

A mixed-up kid.

83 **W**hat do you call a sheep in a bikini?

Bra-bra black sheep.

84 **W**hat do you call a shy sheep?

Baaaashful.

85 **W**hat do you call a snake that works for the
government?

A civil serpent.

86 **W**hat do you call a tall building that pigs work in?

A styscraper.

87 **W**hat
do you
call a
zebra
without
stripes?

A horse.

88 **W**hat do you call cattle that always sit down?

Ground beef.

89 **W**hat do you call the ghost of a chicken?

A poultrygeist.

90 **W**hat do you call two pigs who write letters to each other?

Pen-pals.

91 **W**hat do you do if you come across an unconscious rodent?

Give it mouse to mouse.

92 **W**hat do you do when you see two snails fighting?

Nothing, you just let them slug it out.

93 **W**hat do you get when you cross a corgi with a clock?

A watchdog.

94 **W**hat do you get when you cross a dog with a vegetable?

A jack brussel.

95 **W**hat do you get when you cross a monkey with a flower?

A chimp-pansy.

96 **W**hat do you give to a horse with a sore throat?

Cough stirrup.

97 **W**hat do you give to a sick snake?

An asp-rin.

98 **W**hat do you say to a hitchhiking frog?

Hop in.

99 **W**hat does a lizard wear on special occasions?

A rep-tie.

100 **W**hat does an educated owl say?

Whom.

101 **W**hat game do cows play at parties?

Moosical chairs.

The scene at the party after the cows finished their game of Moosical Chairs and the herd went home

102 **W**hat goes 'oom, oom?'

A cow walking backwards.

103 **W**hat happened to the cat who swallowed a ball of wool?

She had mittens.

104 **W**hat happened when the Big Bad Wolf fell into Grandma's washing machine?

He became a wash and werewolf.

105 **W**hat has an elephant's trunk, a tiger's stripes, a giraffe's neck and a baboon's bottom?

A zoo.

106 **W**hat has four legs and flies?

A dead cat.

107 **W**hat has six legs, bites, buzzes and talks in code?

A morse-quito.

108 **W**hat's a bee's favourite meal?

A humburger.

the hills are alive...
with the sound of mooosic

ON A HILL...SOMEWHERE IN AUSTRIA

109 **W**hat's a cow's favourite film?
'*The Sound of Moosic.*

110 **W**ho is a cow's favourite singer?
Moodonna.

111 **W**hat's a crocodile's favourite game?
Snap.

SNAP
I WIN!

112 **W**hat's a frog's favourite drink?
Croaka-cola.

113 **W**hat's a little fish's favourite TV show?
Plaice School.

114 **W**hat's a pig's favourite ballet?

Swine Lake.

115 **W**hat's a sheep's favourite dessert?

A Mars Baaaaa.

116 **W**ho is a snake's favourite singer?

Wriggley Houston.

117 **W**hat's a tadpole after it is five days old?

Six days old.

118 **W**hat's an army of worms called?

An apple corps.

119 **W**hat's an octopus's favourite song?

'I want to hold your hand, hand, hand, hand, I want to hold your hand, hand, hand, hand.'

120 **W**hat's big and grey and out of bounds?

A tired kangaroo.

121 **W**hat's black and white and red all over?

A sunburned zebra.

122 **W**hat's green and hard?

A frog with a machine gun.

123 **W**hat's grey, has four legs and a trunk?

A mouse going on holiday.

124 **W**hat's Kermit the Frog's middle name?

The.

125 **W**hat's small, brown and squirts jam?

A hamster eating a doughnut.

126 **W**hat's smaller than an ant's mouth?

An ant's dinner.

127 **W**hat's the favourite class for snakes?

Hiss-tory.

128 **W**hat kind of cat loves swimming?

An octopussy.

129 **W**hat kind of doctor treats ducks?

A quack.

130 **W**hat kind of vehicles do pigs drive?

Pig-up trucks.

131 **W**hy should you never kiss chickens?

Because they've got foul breath.

132 **W**hat song do lions sing at Christmas?
Jungle bells.

133 **W**hat type of cats go bowling?
Alley cats

134 **W**hat type of fish is always sleeping?
A kipper.

Do you mind! Can't you see we're trying to get some kip in here!

KIPPERS

135 **W**hat type of food can't tortoises eat?
Fast food.

136 **W**hat's black and white and rolls down a hill?
A penguin.

137 **W**hat's black and white and laughs?
The penguin who pushed the other one.

On the mornings that the worms sleep in . . . .
The early bird misses out on breakfast.

138 **W**hat's the best advice a mother worm can give to her children?
Sleep late.

139 **W**hat's the definition of illegal?
A sick bird.

140 **W**hat's the difference between a bird and a fly?

A bird can fly but a fly can't bird.

141 **W**hat's the difference between a buffalo and a bison?

You can't wash your hands in a buffalo.

142 **W**hat's the healthiest insect?

A vitamin bee.

143 **W**hen is a brown dog not a brown dog?

When it's a greyhound.

144 **W**hen is the best time to buy a canary?

When it's going cheap.

145 **W**here did Noah keep the bees?

In the ark hives.

146 **W**here did the cow go for its holiday?

Moo Zealand.

147 **W**here do baby elephants come from?

Very big storks.

148 **W**here do baby monkeys sleep?

In an apricot.

149 **W**here do chickens go to die?

To oven.

150 **W**here do cows go for entertainment?

The moovies.

151 **W**here do monkeys cook their dinner?

Under the gorilla.

152 **W**here do musical frogs perform?

At the Hopera House.

153 **W**here do pigs go for their holidays?

Hamsterdam.

154 **W**here do pigs go when they die?

To the sty in the sky.

155 **W**here do sheep go on holiday?

Baaaali.

156 **W**here do sheep buy shears?

At a baaaardware store.

157 **W**here do sick ponies go?

To the horsepital.

158 **W**here would you find a dog with no legs?

Exactly where you left it.

159 **W**here would you weigh a whale?

At a whale-weigh station.

160 **W**hich animal never stops talking?

The yak.

161 **W**hich animals are best at maths?

Rabbits, because they're always multiplying.

162 **W**hich area of the police force accepts monkeys?

The Special Branch.

163 **W**hich bird can lift the heaviest weights?

The crane.

164 **W**hich bird never grows up?

The minor bird.

165 **W**hich bird succeeds?

A budgie without teeth.

166 **W**hich hen lays the longest?

A dead one.

167 **W**hich insects can tell the time?

Clockroaches.

168 **W**hich movie character do insects like best?

Bug Lightyear.

169 **W**hy are beavers so smart?

Because they gnaw everything.

170 **W**hich TV show do cows never miss?

The moos.

171 **W**hich TV show do horses like best?

Neigh-bours.

172 **W**hich vegetables have toes at the end?

Tomatoes and potatoes.

173 **W**ho is emperor of all mice?

Julius Cheeser.

174 **W**ho is the most feared animal of all?

Attila the hen.

175 **W**ho is the king of the monkeys?

Henry the Ape.

176 **W**hy are dolphins clever?

Because they live in schools.

177 **W**hy can't frogs get life insurance?

Because they are always croaking.

178 **W**hy can't you have a conversation with a goat?

Because it always butts in.

179 **W**hy can't you play a practical joke on snakes?

Because they don't have a leg to pull.

180 **W**hy did Bo Peep lose her sheep?

She had a crook with her.

181 **W**hy did the bat miss the train?

Because it spent too long hanging around.

182 **W**hy did the cat put the letter 'M' into the freezer?

Because it turns 'ice' into 'mice'.

The chicken that always crosses the road having second thoughts on whether he should cross the busy 6 lane motorway at all...

183 **W**hy did the chicken cross the road, roll in the mud and cross the road again?

Because he was a dirty double-crosser.

184 **W**hy did the chicken join the band?

Because it had drumsticks.

185 **W**hy did the fish cross the sea?

To get to the other tide.

186 **W**hy did the fish jump out of the water?

Because the seaweed.

187 **W**hy did the flies run across the top of the cling wrap box?

Because it read 'Tear along the dotted line.'

188 **W**hy did the frog throw away the book?

Because he'd reddit (read it).

189 **W**hy did the goose cross the road?

To prove it wasn't chicken.

190 **W**hy did the koala fall out of the tree?

Because it was dead.

191 **W**hy did the rooster refuse to fight?

Because he was chicken.

192 **W**hy did the shark take so long to eat a victim's arm?

Because the victim's watch made it time consuming.

193 **W**hy did the termite quit its job?

Because it was boring.

194 **W**hy did the traffic officer book the sheep?

Because it did a ewe turn.

195 **W**hy did the zookeeper refuse to work in the elephant enclosure?

Because the work kept piling up.

196 **W**hy do chickens watch TV?

For hentertainment.

197 **W**hy do frogs like beer?

Because it is made from hops.

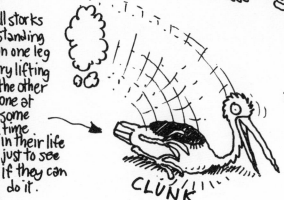

198 **W**hy does a stork stand on one leg?

It would fall over if it lifted the other one.

199 **W**hy does a tiger have stripes?

So it won't be spotted.

200 **W**hy don't anteaters get sick?

Because they're full of ant-ibodies.

201 **W**hy don't cats shave?

Because they prefer Whiskas.

202 **W**hy is the letter 'T' important to a stick insect?

Because without it, it would be a sick insect.

203 **W**hy should you never fight an echidna?

Because she will always win on points.

204 **W**hy was the alligator called Kodak?

Because he was always snapping.

205 **W**hy was the kangaroo mad at her children?

Because they were jumping on the bed.

206 **W**hy was the little bear spoilt?

Because he was panda'd to.

207 **W**hy wasn't the butterfly invited to the dance?

Because it was a moth ball.

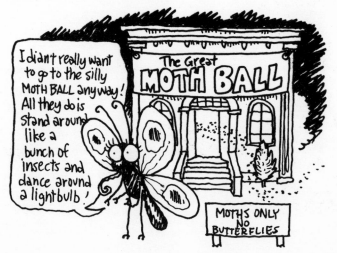

Dinosaurs

208 **H**ow do dinosaurs pass exams?

With extinction.

209 **H**ow do dinosaurs pay their bills?

With Tyrannosaurus Cheques.

210 **H**ow would you feel if you saw a dinosaur in your backyard?

Very old.

211 **W**hat do you call a dinosaur that never gives up?

A try and try and try-ceratops.

212 **W**hen did the last dinosaur die?

After the second-last dinosaur.

213 **W**hat do you cut a dinosaur bone with?

A dino-saw.

214 **W**hat do you get when you cross a dinosaur with a pig?

Jurassic Pork.

215 **W**hat do you get when you cross a dinosaur with explosives?

Dino-mite.

216 **W**hat do you get when you cross a Stegosaurus with a pig?

A porky spine.

217 **W**hat's the hardest part of making dinosaur stew?
Finding a pot big enough to hold the dinosaur.

218 **W**hat's the scariest dinosaur of all?
The Terrordactyl.

219 **W**here do dinosaurs go to the toilet?
In the dino-sewer.

SCARY HEY?

The scariest thing in Prehistoric skies...
The Terrorsaurus

220 **W**hich dinosaur does well in English exams?
Tyrannathesaurus Rex.

221 **W**hich dinosaur was a famous author?
Jane Bronte-saurus.

222 **W**hy are old dinosaur bones kept in a museum?
Because they can't find any new ones.

I think the footbone is connected to the ankle bone...or is it the leg bone?
I know the leg bone is connected to the hip bone...
or is it the knee bone?

MUSEUM

223 **W**hy did the dinosaur cross the road?

Because there were no chickens.

Where does a dinosaur cross a busy 6 Lane motorway? Anywhere it likes!!

224 **W**hy did the dinosaur not cross the road?

It was extinct.

Miscellaneous

225 **W**hat did the big chimney say to the little chimney?

You're too young to smoke.

226 **W**hat did the big telephone say to the little telephone?

You're too young to get engaged.

227 **W**hat did the power point say to the plug?

Socket to me.

228 **W**hat has four wheels and flies?

A garbage truck.

229 **W**hat's red and white?

Pink.

230 **H**ow do fishermen make a net?

They make lots of holes and tie them together with string.

231 **W**hat time do most people go to the dentist?

Tooth-hurty.

232 **W**hat's small and wobbly and sits in a pram?

A jelly baby.

233 **W**hy do artists make lots of money?

Because they can draw their own wages.

234 '**A**re you awake?'

'*No!*'

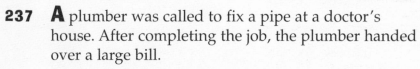

235 '**W**hat's the difference between a marshmallow and a pykost?'

'*What's a pykost?*'

'About two dollars.'

236 '**M**ay I try on that dress in the window?'

'*No. I'm afraid you'll have to use the dressing-room like everyone else.*'

237 **A** plumber was called to fix a pipe at a doctor's house. After completing the job, the plumber handed over a large bill.

'*That's outrageous,*' said the doctor. '*I don't earn that much as a surgeon.*'

'Neither did I when I was a surgeon,' said the plumber.

238 **W**hen do mathematicians die?

When their number's up.

239 **W**hat's the difference between a bus driver and a cold?

One knows the stops, the other stops the nose.

240 **W**hat did the ground say to the rain?

If this keeps up, I'll be mud.

241 **H**ow do you make a Venetian blind?

Poke his eyes out.

242 **W**ho steals from her grandma's house?

Little Red Robin Hood.

243 **W**hat colour is a hiccup?

Burple.

244 **W**hy was the broom late?

It overswept.

245 **'C**an you stand on your head?'

'No, my feet won't reach.'

246 **W**hich king was purple and had many wives?

King Henry the Grape.

247 '**M**y son writes for money.'

'Is he a novelist?'

'No, he's travelling. Every few days I get a letter asking for money.'

248 '**W**here do you come from?'

'Australia.'

'Which part.'

'All of me.'

249 '**W**here's your Mum?'

'On holiday.'

'Jamaica?'

'No, she went of her own accord.'

250 '**W**here's your Mum?'

'On holiday.'

'Jakarta?'

'No, she caught a plane.'

251 **A**irline Steward: 'It is an offence to smoke on an airplane. Anyone caught doing so will be asked to finish it outside.'

252 **H**ow do Eskimos dress?

As quickly as possible.

The Eskimo boy who took too long to get dressed for school one morning

253 **H**ow do you make a Maltese cross?

Hit him on the head.

254 **H**ow much does Uluru (Ayers Rock) weigh?

One stone.

255 What's purple, 5000 years old and 400 kilometres long?

The Grape Wall of China.

256 When is a car not a car?

When it has turned into a driveway.

257 'Where does this road go?'

'Nowhere. It stays right where it is.'

258 Why did the car get a puncture?

There was a fork in the road.

259 What do you call a man with a bus on his head?

Dead.

260 **A** person pushes to the front of an airport queue: 'Excuse me, how long will the flight take?'

Airline Official: *'Just a minute.'*

Person: *'Thank you.'*

261 **A** couple are in an airport queue.

Husband: *'We should have brought the dining room cabinet.'*

Wife: *'Why?'*

Husband: *'That's where I left the tickets.'*

262 **'C**all me a cab.'

'You're a cab.'

263 **'M**y sister just married an Irishman.'

'Oh really.'

'No, O'Reilly.'

264 **W**hen is a match not a match?

When it's alight.

265 **W**hat's that lyin' on the floor?'

'That's no lion, that's an elephant.'

266 **A** horse walks into a bar.

Barman: *'Why the long face?'*

267 **A** termite walks into a bar.

Termite: *'Is the bar tender tonight?'*

268 **A** fish flounders into a bar, its tongue hanging out.

Barman: *'What can I get you?'*

Fish: *'Water, water.'*

269 **T**wo horses are in a bar.

Horse 1: *'I see you had a good win on the track last week.'*

Horse 2: *'Thanks. I'm in pretty good form.'*

270 **A** greyhound walks up to two horses at a bar.

Greyhound: *'Can I buy you both a drink?'*

The horses look at each other in amazement.

Horse 1: *'I didn't know dogs could talk.'*

271 **T**wo chickens walk into a bar.

Barman: *'Sorry, we don't serve food in here.'*

272 **A** man is lost in the desert. He crawls along, getting thirstier and thirstier. A man approaches with a case full of ties. 'Would you like to buy a tie?' the tie salesman asks. 'Water, water' the other man pleads. 'Sorry, I only have ties.' Hours later, with the thirsty man near death, another man approaches. He too has ties but no water. The thirsty man keeps crawling. Almost dead, he sees in the distance a bar. He crawls to the entrance only to be stopped by a bouncer. 'Sorry sir,' the bouncer says. 'You can't get in without a tie.'

273 **A** man walked into a bar.

'*Ouch!*'

274 **A** man walks into a bar with a skunk under his arm.

Barman: '*You can't bring that smelly thing in here.*'

Skunk: '*Sorry. I'll leave him outside.*'

275 **H**ow many animals did Moses fit in the Ark?

None, it was Noah's Ark.

276 **W**here was Noah when the lights went out?

In d'ark.

277 How did Noah steer the Ark at night?

He switched on the floodlights.

278 What did Noah say as he was loading the animals?

'Now I herd everything.'

279 How do we know that Moses was sick?

God gave him tablets.

280 Person 1: 'Pssst. Do you want to buy the genuine skull of Julius Caesar?'

Person 2: *'You sold me his skull last week. Besides, that one is smaller.'*

Person 1: *'This is when he was a boy.'*

281 How did the Vikings send messages?

By Norse code.

282 Customer: 'Have you got William Shakespeare's Hamlet?'

Bookshop owner: *'I don't know. When did he order it?'*

283 Where are English kings and queens crowned?

On the head.

284 Where's Hadrian's Wall?

Around his garden.

285 Who invented the weekend?

Robinson Crusoe—he had all his work done by Friday.

286 Person 1: 'I've never been so insulted in all my life.'

Person 2: *'You haven't been trying.'*

Well my good friend... for 6 long years and 210 days I've been calling you Friday... But I've made a big mistake in my calculation. Your name should be Wednesday...no.... hangabout... there was a public holiday in there ...you're Monday my man! Monday!

287 **H**ome owner: 'Come here. I'll teach you to throw stones at my window.'

Child: *'I already know how.'*

288 **'T**hat dress fits you like a glove. It sticks out in five places.'

289 **W**ho is the smelliest person in the world?

King Pong.

290 **S**heriff: 'You're not allowed to fish here.'

Boy: *'I'm not fishing. I'm giving my pet worm a bath.'*

291 **S**heriff: 'You need a permit to catch fish.'

Boy: *'What's wrong with worms?'*

292 Police officer: 'Can you please blow into this bag.'
Motorist: *'Why, are your chips too hot?'*

293 What do traffic wardens put on their sandwiches?
Traffic jam.

294 Did you hear about the criminal contortionist?
He turned himself in.

295 Why was the baby pen crying?
Because its mum was doing a long sentence.

296 'Officer, someone's stolen my wig.'
'Don't worry, we'll comb the area.'

Madam... we combed the area and found your lost wig sunning itself by the neighbour's pool... and believe me, it didn't come along willingly!

297 Man: 'You were supposed to come around yesterday and fix my doorbell.'

Electrician: 'I did. I rang twice but no one answered.'

298 Did you hear about the unlucky sailor?

First he was shipwrecked, then he was rescued—by the Titanic.

299 Why are gloves clumsy?

Because they're all fingers and thumbs.

300 Why did the snowman dress up?

Because he was going to the snowball.

The snowman who stayed chatting too long at the snowball

301 Mother: 'Don't go too close to the lake. It's very deep.'

Child: *'No it's not. It only goes up to the duck's middle.'*

Stewardess...
Please let the
passengers know
we're about to
come to an abrupt
halt....
Don't use the term
CRASH
It may unsettle
the nervous
passengers!

302 **W**hat happened when the bell fell in the swimming pool?

It got wringing wet.

303 **N**ervous Passenger: 'Do these planes crash often?'

Pilot: *'Only once.'*

304 **A** house was burgled last night. Everything was stolen except for some soap and towels that were on top of a cupboard. Police are looking for some low-down, dirty thieves.

305 **W**hy did the gangster kill his pet pig?

Because it squealed to the police.

306 **H**ow did the comedian pass the time in hospital?

By telling sick jokes.

Hey! Did you hear the joke about the poor guy with two broken arms, a broken leg, a fractured collar bone, a bruised head and one black eye? Well... I'm that guy!

307 **W**hy did the criminals whisper in the meadow?

Because they didn't want to be overheard by the grass.

308 **W**hen is a car like a frog?

When it is being toad.

309 **T**wenty puppies were stolen from a pet shop.

Police are warning people to look out for anyone selling hot dogs.

310 **W**hat's green and pecks on trees?

Woody Wood Pickle.

311 **W**hat wears an anorak and pecks on trees?

Woody Wood Parka.

312 **W**hat did the waterfall say to the fountain?

You're just a little squirt.

313 **W**ho's faster
than a speeding bullet
and full
of food?

Super Market.

314 **W**ho delivers
Christmas presents to
the wrong houses?

Santa Flaws.

315 **W**hich song is top
of the Eskimo hit
parade?

*'There's No Business
Like Snow Business.'*

316 **W**hat wears nine gloves, eighteen shoes and a mask?

A baseball team.

317 How do you get four suits for a couple of dollars?

Buy a pack of cards.

318 What did one elevator say to the other?

'I think I'm coming down with something.'

319 What did one magnet say to the other magnet?

'I find you very attractive.'

320 What did the rug say to the floor?

'Don't move, I've got you covered.'

321 **H**ow do prisoners call home?

On cell phones.

322 **W**hy do bagpipers walk when they play?

They're trying to get away from the noise.

323 **W**hat's Chinese and deadly?

Chop sueycide.

324 **W**hy is it impossible to die of starvation in the desert?

Because of the sand which is there (sandwiches there).

325 **W**hat's big and white and can't jump over a fence?

A fridge.

326 **P**olice have arrested two kids, one for playing with fireworks, and one for stealing a battery. They charged one and let the other one off.

327 **T**he guy who invented the hokey pokey died but they couldn't get him into the coffin. His right leg was in, then his right leg was out, his right leg was …

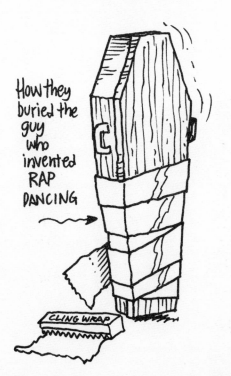

How they buried the guy who invented RAP DANCING

328 **W**ho were the world's shortest lovers?

Gnomeo and Juliet.

329 **W**hat do you get when two prams collide?

A creche.

330 **W**hat are government workers called in Spain?

Seville servants.

331 **H**ow do you make antifreeze?

Lock her outside in the cold.

332 **W**hat did the shoe say to the foot?

You're having me on.

333 **W**ho swings through the cakeshop, yodelling?

Tarzipan.

334 **W**hat did one sole say to the other?

'I think we're being followed by a couple of heels.'

335 **W**hat were the gangster's final words?

'What is that violin doing in my violin case?'

336 **W**hat's the definition of minimum?

A very small mother.

337 Two prisoners escaped from custody. One was seven feet tall, the other four feet. Police searched high and low for them.

338 What illness do retired pilots get?
Flu.

339 When is a door not a door?
When it's ajar.

340 Where do old Volkswagens go?
To the old volks home.

341 Which trees are always sad?
Pine trees.

342 **W**hen is the cheapest time to phone friends?

When they're not home.

343 **H**ow do you clean the sky?

With a skyscraper.

344 **W**hat do you call a bear with no fur?

A bare.

Sure it might be cool for a bear to shave all over and wear boxer shorts in summer... But let's just hope his fur grows back by Winter!

345 **W**hy did the Mexican push his wife over the cliff?

Tequila.

346 **W**hat did the electrician's wife say when he got home?

'Wire you insulate.'

347 **W**hich bus sailed the oceans?

Columbus

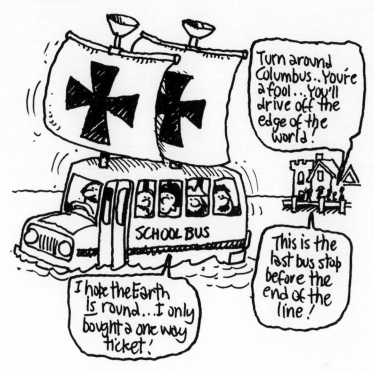

348 **W**hy did Henry VIII have so many wives?

He liked to chop and change.

349 **W**hat did the hat say to the scarf?

You hang around and I'll go ahead.

350 **W**hen does the alphabet only have 24 letters?

When U and I aren't there.

351 **W**hat's the difference between going to church and going to the movies?

At church, they say 'Stand up for Jesus.' At the movies, they shout, 'Sit down for Christ's sake.'

352 Two university professors are sitting on a verandah.

Professor 1: *'Have you read Marx?'*

Professor 2: *'Yes, these cane chairs will do it every time.'*

353 Did Adam and Eve have a date?

No, they had an apple.

354 Where did Captain Cook stand when he landed in Australia?

On his feet.

Monsters, Witches, Ghosts and Vampires

355 Person 1: 'Why are you wearing garlic your neck.'

Person 2: *'It keeps away vampires.'*

Person 1: *'But there are no vampires.'*

Person 2: *'See, it works.'*

356 **A** ghost walks into a bar.

Bartender: *'Sorry, we don't serve spirits here.'*

357 **C**annibal 1: 'How do you make an explorer stew?'

Cannibal 2: *'Keep him waiting a few hours.'*

358 **D**id you hear about the cannibal who gnawed a bone for hours on end?

When he stood up, he fell over.

359 **D**id you hear about the ghosts' running race?

It was a dead heat.

360 **D**id you hear about the vampire who got taken away in a straightjacket?

He went batty.

361 **D**id you hear about the vampire comedian?
He specialised in biting satire.

362 **D**id you hear about the weather wizard?
He's forecasting sunny spells.

363 **D**o zombies like the dark?
Of corpse they do.

364 **H**ow can you tell if a corpse is angry?
It flips its lid.

365 **H**ow can you help a hungry cannibal?
Give him a hand.

366 **H**ow can you tell what a ghost is getting for its birthday?
By feeling its presence.

367 How do you greet a three-headed monster?

'Hello, hello, hello.'

368 How do you greet a six-headed monster?

'I didn't know you were twins.'

369 How do you make a witch itch?

Take away the 'w'.

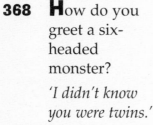

370 How does a yeti feel when it gets a cold?

Abominable.

371 How does Dracula eat his food?

In bite sized pieces.

372 What did Frankenstein do when he saw the monster catcher approaching?

He bolted.

373 **P**olice Officer 1: 'Where's the skeleton?'

Police Officer 2: *'I had to let him go.'*

Police Officer 1: *'But he's our main suspect.'*

Police Officer 2: *'I know. But I couldn't pin anything on him.'*

374 **M**r Cannibal: 'I've brought a friend home for dinner.'

Mrs Cannibal: *'But I've already made a stew.'*

375 **W**hat did the alien say to the plant?

Take me to your weeder.

376 **W**hat did Quasimodo become after he died?

A dead ringer.

377 **W**hat did the alien say to her son when he returned home?

Where on Earth have you been?

378 **W**hat did the cannibal say to the explorer?

'Nice to meat you.'

379 **W**hat did the cannibal say when he saw his wife chopping up a python and a pygmy?

'Yum, snake and pygmy pie.'

380 **W**hat did the cannibal say when he was full?

'I couldn't eat another mortal.'

381 **W**hat did the cannibal say when he saw Dr Livingstone?

'Dr Livingstone, I consume.'

382 **W**hat did the sea monster say when it saw the brand new ocean liner sail past?

'Yum. Launch time.'

383 **W**hat did the ghost buy for his wife?

A see-through nightie.

384 **W**hat do goblin children do after school?

Their gnomework.

385 **W**hat do little zombies play?

Corpses and robbers.

386 **W**hat do monsters have mid-morning?
A coffin break.

387 **W**hat do sea monsters eat?
Fish and ships.

388 **W**hat do the guests do at a cannibal wedding?
Toast the bride and groom.

389 **W**hat do vampire footballers have at half times?
Blood oranges.

390 **W**hat do vegetarian cannibals eat?
Swedes.

391 **W**hat do you call a 12-foot, two-headed monster?

Anything it likes.

392 **W**hat do you call a ghost's mum and dad?

Transparents.

393 **W**hat do you call a detective skeleton?

Sherlock Bones.

394 **W**hat do you call a witch without a broomstick?

A witch-hiker.

395 **W**hat do you do if you're surrounded by a witch, a werewolf, a vampire and two ghosts?

Hope you're at a fancy dress party.

396   **W**hat do you call a hairy beast in a river?

A weir-wolf.

397   **W**hat do you call a skeleton who sits around doing nothing?

Lazy bones.

398   **W**hat do zombies use to make cakes?

Self-raising flour.

399 What do you call a protest march by devils?

A demon-stration.

400 What does a cannibal say when a bus load of tourists drives past?

'Smorgasbord.'

401 What does a monster call his parents?

Dead and mummy.

402 What does a vampire never order at a restaurant?

Stake.

403 What does an undertaker take before starting work?

A stiff drink.

404 **W**hat does a devil do to keep fit?

Exorcise.

405 **W**hat happened to the naughty schoolgirl witch?

She was ex-spelled.

406 **W**hat's a vampire's favourite sport?

Batminton.

407 **W**hat happened when the gravediggers went on strike?

Their job was done by a skeleton crew.

408 **W**hat's a witch's favourite movie?

Broom with a View.

409 **W**hat's Dr Jekyll's favourite game?

Hyde and seek.

410 **W**hat's Dracula's car called?

A mobile blood unit.

411 **W**here does Dracula keep his money?

In the blood bank.

412 **W**ho is a ghost's favourite singer?

Mighoul Jackson.

413 **W**hat kind of plate does a skeleton eat off?

Bone china.

414 **W**hat song did the band play at the Demons and Ghouls ball?

'Demons are a Ghouls Best Friend.'

415 **W**hat trees do ghosts like best?

Ceme-trees.

416 **W**hat type of music do mummies like best?

Ragtime.

417 **W**hat type of music do zombies like best?

Soul music.

418 **W**hat vehicles race at the Witches Formula One Grand Prix?

Vroomsticks.

419 **W**hat was the skeleton rock band called?

The Strolling Bones.

420 **W**hat was the wizard's favourite band?

ABBA-cadabra.

421 **W**hat's a vampire's favourite dance?

The fangdango.

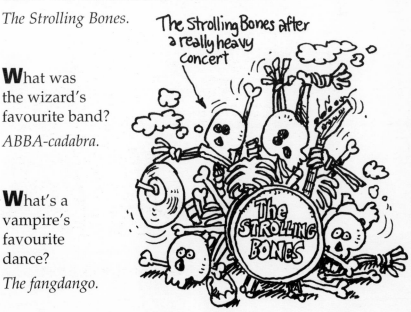

422 What's the favourite game at a cannibal's birthday party?

Swallow the leader.

423 What's three metres tall, has 12 fingers and three eyes and wears sunglasses?

A monster on its summer holiday.

424 What's a skeleton's favourite musical instrument?

A trom-bone.

425 Where do Australian ghosts live?

In the Northern Terror-tory.

426 Where do cannibals work?

At head office.

427 **W**here do ghosts go swimming?

In the dead sea.

428 **W**hich ghost is President of France?

Charles de Ghoul.

429 **W**hich ghost ate the three bears' porridge?

Ghouldilocks.

430 **W**ho did the witch call when her broom was stolen?

The flying squad.

431 **W**ho finished last at the Yeti Olympics?

Frosty the Slowman.

432 **W**ho is big and hairy, wears a dress and climbs the Empire State Building?

Queen Kong.

433 **W**ho is King of the Cannibals?

Henry the Ate.

434 **W**ho is the King of the Wizards?

William the Conjurer.

435 **W**hy are Cyclops couples happy together?

Because they always see eye to eye.

436 **W**hy are ghosts always tired?

Because they are dead on their feet.

437 **W**ho won the running race between Count Dracula and Countess Dracula?

It was neck and neck.

438 **W**hy couldn't the witch race her horse in the Witches Derby?

Because it was having a spell.

439 **W**hy did the cannibal eat the missionary?

Because he'd developed a taste for Christianity.

440 **W**hy did the cannibal kidnap the tourist?

He wanted take-away.

441 **W**hy did the cannibal live on his own?

He'd had his fill of other people.

442 **W**hy did the demon jump into the conserve?

Because he was a jammy devil.

443 **W**hy did the vampire go to the orthodontist?

To improve his bite.

444 **W**hy did the executioner go to work early?

To get a head start.

445 **W**hy did the young vampire follow his dad's profession?

Because it was in his blood.

446 **W**hy did the witches go on strike?

Because they wanted sweeping reforms.

447 **W**hy didn't the skeleton bother to defend itself in court?

Because it didn't have a leg to stand on.

448 **W**hy didn't the skeleton want to go to work?

Because his heart wasn't in it.

449 **W**hy do ghosts like the Spice Girls?

Because they're an all ghoul band.

450 **W**hy do ghosts speak Latin?

Because it's a dead language.

451 **W**hy do skeletons drink milk?

Because it's good for the bones.

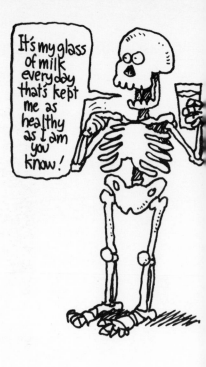

452 **W**hy do skeletons hate winter?

Because the wind just goes straight through them.

453 **W**hy do vampires play poker?

Because they like playing for high stakes.

454 **W**hy do witches get good bargains?

Because they're good at haggling.

455   **W**hy don't cannibals eat weather forecasters?
Because they give them wind.

456   **W**here do you find a skeleton's address?
In the bone book.

457   **W**hy is Count Dracula skinny?
Because he eats necks to nothing.

458   **W**hy isn't the Abominable Snowman scared of people?
Because he doesn't believe in them.

Doctor, Doctor

459 Doctor, doctor, how long have I got?

10.

10 what? 10 months? 10 weeks?

10, 9, 8, 7 …

460 Doctor, doctor, how was my check up?

Perfect. You'll live to be 80.

But I am 80.

In that case, it's been nice knowing you.

461 Doctor, doctor, have you got something for a migraine?

Take this hammer and hit yourself on the head.

462 Doctor, doctor, I ate some oysters and now I'm feeling sick.

Were they fresh?

How can you tell?

You open the shell and have a look.

You're not supposed to eat the shell?

463 Doctor, doctor, I think I might croak.

It's just a frog in your throat.

AAARGHH! If that's having a frog in your throat... ...I'd hate to be feeling a little hoarse !!

464 Doctor, doctor, I can't feel my legs.

That's because we had to amputate your arms.

465 Doctor, doctor, I came as quick as I could. What's the problem?

Your lab results are back and you've only got 24 hours to live.

That's terrible.

There's worse. I've been trying to call you since yesterday.

466 Doctor, doctor, I feel like a bird.

I'll tweet you in a minute.

467 Doctor, doctor, I feel like a strawberry.

I can see you're in a bit of a jam.

468 Doctor, doctor, I keep seeing double.

Please sit on the couch.

Which one?

469 Doctor, doctor, I've lost all my hair.

That's a bald statement.

470 Doctor, doctor, I keep thinking I'm a fish.

You've got water on the brain.

471 **D**octor, doctor, I keep seeing green aliens with two heads and four legs.

Have you seen a psychiatrist?

No, just green aliens with two heads and four legs.

472 **D**octor, doctor, I need something for my temper.

Just wait 'til you get the bill.

473 **D**octor, doctor, I keep thinking I'm a donut.

Let's talk about this over coffee.

474 **D**octor, doctor, I swallowed a whole cantaloupe.

You're just feeling melon-choly.

475 **D**octor, doctor, my hands are killing me.

Take them off your throat.

476 **D**octor, doctor, I think I'm a clock.

You're winding me up.

477 **D**octor, doctor, I think I'm losing my mind.

Don't worry, you won't miss it.

478 **D**octor, doctor, I think I'm turning into a woman.

Well, you are 16 now Amanda.

479 **D**octor, doctor, I think I'm suffering from déjà vu.

Haven't I seen you before?

480 Doctor, doctor, I've got a terrible cold. What should I do?

Go home, take a hot bath then stand outside in the cold with no clothes on.

But if I do that, I'll get pneumonia.

That's the idea. I can treat pneumonia. I can't treat a cold.

481 Doctor, doctor, I've lost my memory.

When did this happen?

When did what happen?

482 Doctor, doctor, if I give up wine, women and song, will I live longer?

No, but it will seem longer.

483 Doctor, doctor, I've got jelly in my ear.

You're just a trifle deaf.

484 Doctor, doctor, my baby's swallowed some explosives.

Well don't annoy him. We don't want him to go off.

485 Doctor, doctor, my hands won't stop shaking.

Do you drink a lot?

No, most of it spills.

486 Doctor, doctor, my son swallowed my razor-blade.

Well just use your electric razor.

487 Doctor, doctor, my wife's contractions are only five minutes apart.

Is this her first child?

No, this is her husband.

488 Doctor, doctor, should I file my nails?

No, throw them away like everyone else does.

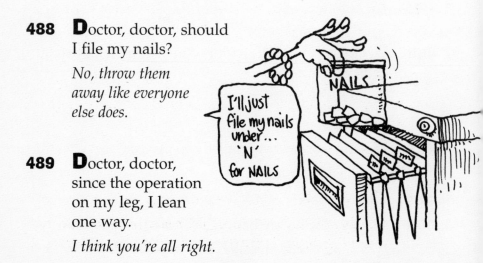

489 Doctor, doctor, since the operation on my leg, I lean one way.

I think you're all right.

490 Doctor, doctor, sometimes I feel like a goat.

How long has this been going on?

Ever since I was a kid.

Even as a child... Bernard was always different from the other kids.

491 Doctor, doctor, sometimes I feel like an onion and sometimes I feel like a cucumber.

You've got yourself in a bit of a pickle.

492 Doctor, doctor, sometimes I think I'm a biscuit.

You're crackers.

493 Doctor, doctor, you've taken out my tonsils, my appendix, my gall bladder and one of my kidneys but I still feel sick.

That's enough out of you.

494 Doctor, doctor, what's wrong with me?

Well, you've got a carrot up your nose, a bean in one ear and a French fry in the other. I'd say you're not eating properly.

495 **D**octor, doctor, sometimes I think there are two of me.

Good, you can pay both bills on the way out.

496 **D**octor, doctor, tell me straight. Is it bad?

Just don't start watching any new TV serials.

497 **D**octor, doctor, will I be able to play the violin when my hand heals.

Of course.

Great. Because I couldn't play it before.

498 **D**octor, doctor, I keep seeing spots.

Have you seen an optometrist?

No, just spots.

Food Glorious Food

499 **W**aiter, how did this fly in my soup?

I guess it flew.

500 **W**aiter, I can't eat this meal. Fetch me the manager.

It's no use. He won't eat it either.

501 **W**aiter, do you have frogs' legs.

Yes sir.

Then hop to the kitchen and fetch me a steak.

502 **W**aiter, I'd like burnt steak and soggy chips with a grimy, bitter salad.

I'm afraid the chef won't cook that for you, sir.

Why not? He did yesterday.

503 **W**aiter, I'll have the burger please.

With pleasure.

No, with fries.

504 **W**aiter, I'll have the lamb chops. And make them lean.

Certainly sir. To the right or the left?

505 **W**aiter, is there any soup on the menu?

No madam, I've wiped it all off.

SALAD DIRT

506 **W**aiter, I'll have the soup and the fish please.

I would recommend you eat the fish first. It's been sitting around for a few days and is starting to pong.

507 **W**aiter, there's a cockroach in my soup.

Sorry sir, we're all out of flies.

508 **W**aiter, is this beef or lamb?

Can't you taste the difference?

No.

Then it doesn't matter.

509 **W**aiter, remove this fly now.

But he hasn't finished yet.

510 **W**aiter, there's a dead fly swimming in my soup.

There can't be, sir. Dead flies can't swim.

511 **W**aiter, there's a flea in my soup.

Tell him to hop it.

512 **W**aiter, there's a fly in my soup.

I find that hard to believe sir. The chef used them all in the casserole.

513 **W**aiter, there's a fly in my soup.

No sir, that's a cockroach. The fly's on your roll.

514 **W**aiter, there's a fly in my soup.

That's because the chef used to be a tailor.

515 **W**aiter, there's a fly in my soup.

Would you prefer him in your main course?

516 **W**aiter, there's a fly on my steak.

That's because it's attracted to rotting meat.

517 **W**aiter, there's a spider in my soup.

It must have eaten the fly.

518 **W**aiter, this crab has only got one claw.

It must have been in a fight.

Then bring me the winner.

519 **W**aiter, this coffee tastes like mud.

I can't understand why. It was ground just a minute ago.

520 **W**aiter, we'll have two coffees please. And I want a clean cup.

Yes sir. … Here are your two coffees. Now which one of you wanted the clean cup?

521 **W**aiter, what do you call this dish?

Chicken surprise.

But I can't see any chicken?

That's the surprise.

522 **W**aiter, what's this in my soup.

I don't know, sir. All bugs look the same to me.

523 **W**aiter there's a fly in my soup.

Well you did order fly soup, ma'am.

524 **W**aiter, what kind of soup is this?

Bean soup.

I don't care what it's been. What is it now?

525 **'C**an I have an ice-cream for my little boy?'

'I'd prefer it if you gave me money.'

526 **H**ow do you make a banana split?

Cut it in half.

527 **H**ow do you make a French fry?

Leave him in the sun.

528 **H**ow do you make
a fruit punch?

Give it boxing lessons.

529 **H**ow do you make
a strawberry shake?

Tell it a scary story.

530 **H**ow do you make
a swiss roll?

Push him down a hill.

A punch-up at the Punch Bowl

531 **H**ow do you make an apple crumble?

Smash it with a mallet.

532 **H**ow do you make an egg laugh?

Tell it a yolk.

533 **H**ow do you make a cream puff?

Make it run around the block.

Bob...the lazier of the two rice puddings was down on his training so kept losing his spoon ... then lagged behind at the finish, which eventually lost him the pudding race.

534 How do you start a race between two rice puddings?

Sago.

535 What did the mayonnaise say to the fridge?

'Close the door, I'm dressing.'

536 What do fishermen eat at Easter?

Oyster eggs.

537 What do you call banana skins that you wear on your feet?

Slippers.

538 What do you call two rows of vegetables?

A dual cabbageway.

539 What's a lawyer's favourite dessert?

Suet.

540 What's rhubarb?

Embarrassed celery.

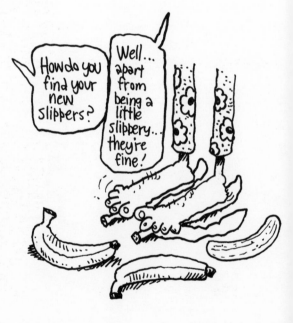

541 **W**hat do you call an egg in the jungle?

An eggsplorer.

542 **W**hat's yellow and square?

A tomato in disguise.

543 **W**hat vegetable can you play snooker with?

A cue-cumber.

544 **W**hat's red, white and brown and travels faster than the speed of sound?

An astronaut's ham and tomato sandwich.

545 **W**hat's too scared to be eaten?

Chicken soup.

546 **W**hich cheese is made backwards?

Edam.

If an egg in the jungle is called an EGGSPLORER, What do you call an egg under an explorer's boot?

SQUASHED!

Boy! That shooting star sure smells like burning ham ... and burning tomato!

It must be an astronaut's ham and tomato sandwich being toasted as it re-enters the Earth's atmosphere!

547 **W**hat's small, round, white and giggles?

A tickled onion.

548 **W**hy did the tomato blush?

Because it saw the salad dressing.

549 **W**hy do gingerbread men wear trousers?

Because they have crummy legs.

550 **W**hy do watermelons get married?

Because they can't-elope.

551 **W**hy does steak taste better in space?

Because it is meteor.

552 **W**hy don't nuts go out at night?

Because they don't want to be assaulted.

Gross Out

553 '**D**octor, can a kid pull out his own tonsils.'
'*Certainly not.*'
'See Jimmy, I told you. Now put them back.'

554 '**I** just got a bunch of flowers for my wife.'
'*Great swap.*'

555 **M**ummy mummy, I don't want to go to New Zealand.

Shut up and keep swimming.

556 **M**ummy mummy, dad has been run over by a steamroller.

Shut up and slide him under the door.

557 **M**ummy mummy, daddy's on fire.

Hurry up and get the marshmallows.

558 **M**ummy mummy, my head hurts.

Shut up and get away from the dart board.

559 **M**ummy mummy, why do I keep going round in circles?

Shut up or I'll nail your other foot to the floor.

560 **M**ummy mummy, what's a vampire?

Shut up and eat your soup before it clots.

561 **M**ummy, mummy, are you sure you bake bread this way?

Shut up and get back in. I can't close the oven door.

562 **M**ummy, mummy, can I play with Rover?

We've already dug him up three times this week.

563 **M**ummy, mummy, dad's going out.

Shut up and throw some more petrol on him.

564 **M**ummy, mummy, daddy just put Rover down.

I'm sure he had a good reason for it.

But he promised I could do it.

565 **M**ummy, mummy, daddy's hammering on the roof again.

Shut up and drive a bit faster.

566 **M**ummy, mummy, I can't find the dog's food.

Shut up and eat your stew.

567 **M**ummy, mummy, I feel like a yo-yo.

Shut up and sit down … and down … and down…

568 **M**ummy, mummy, I hate my brother's guts.

Shut up and eat what's on your plate.

569 **M**ummy, mummy, I'm 16 years old. Don't you think I'm old enough to wear a bra now?

Shut up George.

570 **M**ummy, mummy, sis has got a bruise.

Shut up and eat around it.

571 **M**ummy, mummy, when are we going to have Grandma for dinner?

Shut up. We haven't finished eating your father yet.

572 **M**ummy, mummy, what are you doing with that ax?

Shut up and put your father's leg in the fridge.

573 **M**ummy, mummy, I've just chopped my foot off.

Then hop out of the kitchen, I've just mopped the floor.

574 **M**ummy, mummy, why are we pushing the car off the cliff?

Shut up or you'll wake your father.

575 **M**ummy, mummy, why can't we give Grandma a proper burial?

Shut up and keep flushing.

576 **M**ummy, mummy, why is dad running in zig zags?

Shut up and keep shooting.

577 **M**ummy, mummy, why can't we buy a garbage disposal unit?

Shut up and keep chewing.

578 **D**id you hear the joke about the fart?

It stinks.

579 **S**omeone stole all the toilet seats from the police station.

The officers have nothing to go on.

580 **T**eacher: 'How was your holiday, Penny?'

Penny: *'Great. My brother and I spent the whole time on the beach, burying each other in the sand.'*

Teacher: 'That sounds like fun.'

Penny: *'Daddy says we can go back next year and find him.'*

581 What baseball position did the boy with no arms or legs play?

Home base.

582 What did the first mate see in the toilet?

The captain's log.

583 What do you call a boy who eats his mother and his father?

An orphan.

584 Three kids were playing in a park when a genie appeared. The genie said they could have one wish each, so long as they made the wish while coming down the slide. The first kid slid down shouting 'I want a big glass of lemonade.' The second kid slid down shouting 'I want a chocolate milkshake.' The third kid slid down shouting 'Weeeeee.'

585 What do Eskimos get from sitting on the ice too long?

Polaroids.

586 What's black and white and red all over?

A nun in a blender.

587 **W**hat's twenty metres long and smells of wee?
Line dancing at the old people's home.

588 **W**hat has four legs and an arm?
A happy lion.

On this tour of the African Plain you need to keep your eyes peeled for lions in long grass... scorpions under rocks... stampeding elephants... herds of wild wildebeasts... and of course Giraffe boogie in trees!

589 **W**hat's green and slimy and hangs from trees?
Giraffe boogie.

590 **W**hat's green, has two legs and sits on the end of your finger?
The boogieman.

591 **W**hat's Mozart up to now?
Decomposing.

592 **W**hat's thick and black and picks its nose?
Crude oil.

593 **W**hat's the difference between an oral thermometer and a rectal thermometer?
The taste.

594 Where do lepers shop?

At the secondhand store.

595 Why did the boy take his own toilet paper to the birthday party?

Because he was a party pooper.

596 Why do farts smell?

So that deaf people can appreciate them as well.

597 Why don't elephants pick their nose?

Because they don't know what to do with a 20 kilogram boogie.

598 Why was the sailor buried at sea?

Because he was dead.

599 Woman 1: 'Your son is terribly spoiled.'

Woman 2: *'How dare you. He's not spoiled at all.'*

Woman 1: 'Yes he is. He just got hit by a bus.'

Silly

Inventions

600 **A** chocolate teapot.

601 **A** fly screen on a submarine.

602 **A** glass baseball bat.

603 **A** mirror for ghosts.

604 **A** lead balloon.

605 **A** solar-powered torch.

606 **An** ashtray for a motorbike.

AHRRR! There's nothing there! This mirror's going back ...it doesn't work!

607 **B**lack windows.

608 **R**ubber nails.

609 **N**on-stick glue.

610 **S**ugar cube fishing bait.

611 **U**nderwear for kilt wearers.

612 **A** bikini for Eskimos.

Knock Knock

613 **K**nock knock.
Who's there?
A Fred.
A Fred who?
Who's a Fred of the Big Bad Wolf?

614 **K**nock knock.
Who's there?
Acute.
Acute who?
Acute little boy.

615 **K**nock knock.
Who's there?
Adder.
Adder who?
Adder you get in here?

Adder you get in here?

Well actually... as you'd say in one of your silly 'knock-knock jokes ...I'm trying to get adder here'!

616 **K**nock knock.

Who's there?

Aesop.

Aesop who?

Aesop I saw a puddy cat.

617 **K**nock knock.

Who's there?

Albert.

Albert who?

Albert you don't know who this is?

618 **K**nock knock.

Who's there?

Ahab.

Ahab who?

Ahab to go to the toilet now. Quick open the door.

619 **K**nock knock.

Who's there?

Althea.

Althea who?

Althea later, alligator.

620 **K**nock knock.
Who's there?
Bassoon.
Bassoon who?
Bassoon things will be better.

621 **K**nock knock.
Who's there?
Bea.
Bea who?
Because I'm worth it.

622 **K**nock knock.
Who's there?
Beezer.
Beezer who?
Beezer black and yellow and make honey.

623 **K**nock knock.
Who's there?
Bean.
Bean who?
Bean to any movies lately?

624 **K**nock knock.
Who's there?
Ben Hur.
Ben Hur who?
Ben Hur almost an hour so let me in.

Bees go BUZZ BUZZ Not KNOCK KNOCK!

625 **K**nock knock.

Who's there?

Cattle.

Cattle who?

Cattle always purr when you stroke it.

626 **K**nock knock.

Who's there?

Beth.

Beth who?

Beth wisheth,
thweetie.

Just because you stroke a cat and it purrs...
doesn't mean a cow will do it too.'

627 **K**nock knock.

Who's there?

Burglar.

Burglar who?

Burglars don't knock.

628 **K**nock knock.

Who's there?

Cecil.

Cecil who?

Cecil have music
where ever she goes.

629 **K**nock knock.

Who's there?

Cash.

Cash who?

Are you a nut!

630 **K**nock knock.

Who's there?

Celeste.

Celeste who?

Celeste time I come round here.

631 **K**nock knock.

Who's there?

Cheese.

Cheese who?

Cheese a jolly good fellow.

632 **K**nock knock.

Who's there?

Colin.

Colin who?

Colin all cars. Colin all cars.

633 **K**nock knock.

Who's there?

Cook.

Cook who?

Look at the time, it's one o'clock.

634 **K**nock knock.

Who's there?

Curry.

Curry who?

Curry me back home please.

635 **K**nock knock.
Who's there?
Dan.
Dan who?
Dan Druff.

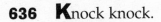

636 **K**nock knock.
Who's there?
Danielle.
Danielle who?
Danielle so loud, I can hear you.

637 **K**nock knock.
Who's there?
Daryl.
Daryl who?
Daryl never be another you.

638 **K**nock knock.
Who's there?
Datsun.
Datsun who?
Datsun old joke.

639 **K**nock knock.
Who's there?
Dish.
Dish who?
Dish is a stick-up.

640 **K**nock knock.
Who's there?
Doris.
Doris who?
The Doris locked so let me in.

641 **K**nock knock.
Who's there?
Dozen.
Dozen who?
Dozen anyone know who I am?

642 **K**nock knock.
Who's there?
Ears.
Ears who?
Ears some more knock
knock jokes.

643 **K**nock knock.
Who's there?
Eddie.
Eddie who?
Eddie body home?

644 **K**nock knock.
Who's there?
Effie.
Effie who?
Effie'd known you were coming he'd have stayed
at home.

645 **K**nock knock.

Who's there?

Eliza.

Eliza who?

Eliza wake at night thinking about you.

Eliza wake thinking about you all night...every night!

646 **K**nock knock.

Who's there?

Evan.

Evan who?

Evan you should know who I am.

647 **K**nock knock.

Who's there?

Fanny.

Fanny who?

Fanny the way you keep asking 'Who's there?'

Fangs for opening the door Igor, It's 5 seconds to sunrise... So slam it shut behind me!

648 **K**nock knock.

Who's there?

Fang.

Fang who?

Fangs for opening the door.

649 **K**nock knock.
Who's there?
Fantasy.
Fantasy who?
Fantasy a walk
on the beach.

650 **K**nock knock.
Who's there?
Ferdie.
Ferdie who?
Ferdie last time open the door.

651 **K**nock knock.
Who's there?
Figs.
Figs who?
Figs the doorbell, it's been broken for ages.

652 **K**nock knock.
Who's there?
Galway.
Galway who?
Galway, you're
annoying me.

653 **K**nock knock.

Who's there?

Fozzie.

Fozzie who?

Fozzie hundredth time, my name is Nick.

654 **K**nock knock.

Who's there?

Germany.

Germany who?

Germany people knock on your door?

655 **K**nock knock.

Who's there?

Haden.

Haden who?

Haden seek.

656 **K**nock knock.

Who's there?

Hugo.

Hugo who?

Hugo one way, I'll go the other.

657 **K**nock knock.

Who's there?

Hy.

Hy who?

(sings) Hy ho, hi ho, it's off to work we go.

658 **K**nock knock.

Who's there?

Ida.

Ida who?

Ida know why I love you like I do.

659 **K**nock knock.

Who's there?

Igloo.

Igloo who?

(sings) Igloo knew Suzie like I know Suzie.

660 **K**nock knock.

Who's there?

Ivor.

Ivor who?

Ivor you let me in or I'll break the door down.

661 **K**nock knock.

Who's there?

Java.

Java who?

Java dollar you can lend me?

662 **K**nock knock.

Who's there?

Jeff.

Jeff who?

Jeff in one ear,
can you please
speak a bit
louder.

663 **K**nock knock.

Who's there?

Kay.

Kay who?

Kay sera sera.

664 **K**nock knock.

Who's there?

Knee.

Knee who?

Knee-d you ask?

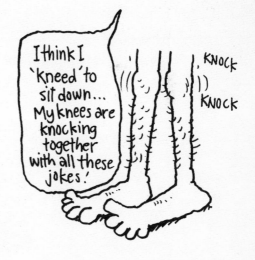

665 **K**nock knock.

Who's there?

Knock knock.

Who's there?

Knock knock.

Who's there?

I'm sorry, but mum told me never to speak to
strangers.

666 **K**nock knock.
Who's there?
Ken.
Ken who?
Ken I come in, it's freezing out here.

667 **K**nock knock.
Who's there?
Lass.
Lass who?
Are you a cowboy?

Of course I'm a real cowboy! I've got all the right gear... the hat... the boots... the lasso... WOH! My line dancing class is starting pardner .... got to go!

668 **K**nock knock.
Who's there?
Lena.
Lena who?
Lena little closer and I'll tell you.

669 **K**nock knock.
Who's there?
Larva.
Larva who?
I larva you.

Come over here Lena ...I've got something important to tell you!

AHHRR!

KNOCK KNOCK

670 **K**nock knock.
Who's there?
Liz.
Liz who?
Lizen carefully to what I have to say.

671 **K**nock knock.

Who's there?

Major.

Major who?

Major answer a
knock knock joke.

672 **K**nock knock.

Who's there?

Mandy.

Mandy who?

Mandy lifeboats, we're sinking.

673 **K**nock knock.

Who's there?

Mary Lee.

Mary Lee who?

(sings) Mary Lee, Mary Lee, Mary Lee, Mary Lee,
Life is but a dream.

674 **K**nock knock.

Who's there?

May.

May who?

May I come in?

675 **K**nock knock.

Who's there?

Maybelle.

Maybelle who?

Maybelle doesn't work either.

676 **K**nock knock.

Who's there?

Moira.

Moira who?

(sings) Moira see you, Moira want you.

677 **K**nock knock.

Who's there?

Nana.

Nana who?

Nana your business.

678 **K**nock knock.

Who's there?

Nobody.

Nobody who?

No body, just a skeleton.

679 **K**nock knock.

Who's there?

Nicholas.

Nicholas who?

Nicholas girls shouldn't climb trees.

680 **K**nock knock.

Who's there?

Neil.

Neil who?

Neil down and take a look through the letter slot.

681 **K**nock knock.

Who's there?

Offer.

Offer who?

Offer gotten who I am.

682 **K**nock knock.

Who's there?

Olive.

Olive Who?

Olive in that house across the road.

683 **K**nock knock.

Who's there?

Olivia.

Olivia who?

Olivia but I've lost my key.

684 **K**nock knock.

Who's there?

Omar.

Omar who?

Omar goodness gracious, I've got the wrong address.

Mum...who's the strange man eating my dinner?

I have no idea son...I think he's got the wrong address

685 **K**nock knock.
Who's there?
Ralph.
Ralph who?
Ralph! Ralph!
Ralph! I'm a dog.

686 **K**nock knock.
Who's there?
Passion.
Passion who?
Just passion by and I thought I'd say hello.

687 **K**nock knock.
Who's there?
Patrick.
Patrick who?
Patricked me into coming over.

688 **K**nock knock.
Who's there?
Razor.
Razor who?
Razor hands, this is a
stick up.

689 **K**nock knock.
Who's there?
Rhoda.
Rhoda who?
(sings) Row, Row, Rhoda boat.

690 **K**nock knock.

Who's there?

Rose.

Rose who?

Rose early to come and see you.

WOH!
Hold on ... we're
entering the
asteroid belt of the
backyard!

691 **K**nock knock.

Who's there?

Roxanne.

Roxanne who?

Roxanne pebbles are all over your garden.

692 **K**nock knock.

Who's there?

Sam.

Sam who?

Sam person who knocked yesterday.

693 **K**nock knock.

Who's there?

Sarah.

Sarah who?

Sarah doctor in the house? I don't feel so good.

Oh Sarah... I don't feel so good!
Call a doctor!
It must be your cooking!

694 **K**nock knock.
Who's there?
Seymour.
Seymour who?
You'll Seymour if you look through the window.

695 **K**nock knock.
Who's there?
Sibyl.
Sibyl who?
Sibyl Simon met a pieman going to the fair.

696 **K**nock knock.
Who's there?
Sigrid.
Sigrid who?
Sigrid Service, now do
exactly as I say.

The ultimate
KNOCK KNOCK
JOKE

BAM

697 **K**nock knock.
Who's there?
Spell.
Spell who?
W.H.O.

698 **K**nock knock.
Who's there?
Stan.
Stan who?
Stan back. I'm going to break the door down.

699 **K**nock knock.
Who's there?
Tex.
Tex who?
Tex two to tango.

700 **K**nock knock.
Who's there?
Thistle.
Thistle who?
Thistle be the last time I knock.

701 **K**nock knock.
Who's there?
Turner.
Turner who?
Turner round and you'll get a better look.

702 **K**nock knock.
Who's there?
Tibet.
Tibet who?
Early Tibet, early to rise.

703 **K**nock knock.
Who's there?
Toyota.
Toyota who?
Toyota be a law against knock knock jokes.

704 **K**nock knock.

Who's there?

Vaughan.

Vaughan who?

Vaughan day
you'll let me in.

705 **K**nock knock.

Who's there?

Vault.

Vault who?

(sings) Vault-sing Matilda.

706 **K**nock knock.

Who's there?

Wanda.

Wanda who?

Wanda buy some cookies?

707 **K**nock knock.
Who's there?
Watson.
Watson who?
Watson TV
tonight?

708 **K**nock knock.
Who's there?
Waddle.
Waddle who?
Waddle you give me to leave you alone.

709 **K**nock knock.
Who's there?
Wenceslas.
Wenceslas who?
Wenceslas bus home?

710 **K**nock knock.
Who's there?
Who.
Who who?
I can hear an echo.

711 **K**nock knock.
Who's there?
You.
You who?
Did you call?

712 **K**nock knock.

Who's there?

Yah.

Yah who?

Ride 'em cowboy.

Riddles and Teasers

713 **W**hen is a bird not a bird?

When it's aloft.

714 **W**ho gets the sack every time he goes to work?

The postman.

715 **W**hat is a prickly pear?

Two hedgehogs.

KISS ME HERE... OUCH!
Try there... OUCH!
Maybe here... OUCH!

Let's just hold hands!

HEDGEHOGS IN LOVE

716 **W**hat has no legs but can walk?

A pair of shoes.

717 **W**hat runs down the street but has no legs?

The kerb.

718 **W**hich word if pronounced right is wrong and if pronounced wrong is right?

Wrong.

719 **H**ow do you make a pair of trousers last?

Make the coat first.

720 **W**hat goes around the house and in the house but never touches the house.

The sun.

With a coat like this... who needs trousers!

721 **W**hat is round and deep but could not be filled up by all the water in the world?

A colander.

722 The more you take, the more you leave behind. What am I?

Footsteps.

723 What is put on a table and cut but never eaten?

A pack of cards.

724 What is the longest word in the world?

Smiles, because there is a mile between the beginning and the end.

725 What has eyes but cannot see?

A potato.

726 What is at the end of the world?

The letter 'D'.

727 **W**hat has ears but cannot hear?

A field of corn.

728 **W**hat starts working only when it's fired?

A rocket.

729 **W**hat burns longer, a 10 centimetre candle or a 20 centimetre candle?

Neither, they both burn shorter.

730 **D**oes a death adder die if it bites its own tongue?

731 **I**f a 7-11 is open 24 hours a day, 365 days a year, why are there locks on the doors?

732 Can a snail have houseguests?

733 If olive oil is made from olives and peanut oil is made from peanuts, what is baby oil made from?

734 Is it easier to break the long jump world record in a leap year?

735 If nothing ever sticks to Teflon, how does Teflon stick to the pan?

736 What was the best thing before sliced bread?

737 What can you hold but never touch?
A conversation.

738 **W**hat did Tennessee?

The same thing Arkansas.

739 **W**hat's the centre of gravity?

The letter 'V'.

740 **W**hat clothes does a house wear?

Address.

741 **W**here does Friday come before Wednesday?

In the dictionary.

742 **W**hat do you call a man who shaves fifteen times a day?

A barber.

It takes 15 shaves a day to keep my face as smooth as this Oh...and a box of sticking plaster a bottle of antiseptic...and a good first aid kit...

743 **I**f a butcher is two metres tall and has size 11 feet, what does he weigh?

Meat.

What do you call ...

744 ... a man who is always around when you need him?
Andy.

745 ... a man with a rug on his head?
Matt.

746 ... a woman with one foot on each side of a river?
Bridget.

747 ... a man floating in the sea?
Bob.

748 ... a man who drives a truck?
Laurie.

749 … a Russian gardener?

Ivanhoe.

750 … a woman who can balance a bottle of beer on her head?

Beatrix.

751 … a woman who gambles?

Betty.

752 … a man with beef, gravy and vegetables on his head?

Stu

753 … a German barber?

Herr Dresser.

754 … a man sitting in a tree?

Woody.

755 … a woman who climbs up walls?

Ivy.

756 What will Bob the Builder be called when he retires?

Bob.

Silly Book Titles

757 'Can't Sleep at Night' by Constance Snoarer

758 'Chinese Lanterns' by Eric Trician

759 'Confessions of a Thief' by I. Dunnit

760 'Eclipse of the Sun' by Ray Oflight

761 'Falling from a Height' by Eileen Toofar

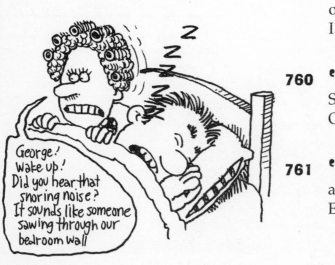

George! Wake up! Did you hear that snoring noise? It sounds like someone sawing through our bedroom wall

762 'Fighting off Burglars' by Al Sayshun

763 'Holiday on the Beach' by Sandy Shaw

Within minutes... the day at the beach became a swim in the ocean....

764 'Housing Problem' by Rufus Quick

765 'Keeping Warm at Night' by Ida Down

766 'Maths for Beginners' by Algy Brar

Dad... do we have a housing problem?

No son... we have a tent problem!

The last time I heard a PING like that... my pants fell down... I dare not look down

PING

767 'Pants Down' by Lucy Lastic

768 'Modern Policing' by U. R. Nicked

769 'My Holiday with the Penguins' by Anne Tarctic

770 '**M**y Life as a Jockey' by Rhoda Horse

771 '**S**winging from the Trees' by Bab Boone

772 '**T**he Arabian Cookbook' by Sultan Vinegar

773 '**T**he Long Sleep' by Anna Sthetic

774 '**T**he Rag and Bone Trade' By Orson Cart

775 '**T**own Planning' by Sir Veyor

776 '**W**ildcats in Sweden' by Bjorn Free

Classroom Capers

777 '**D**ad, can you write in the dark?'

'*I suppose so.*'

'Good. Can you sign my report card, please?'

778 '**D**ad, I's been expelled.'

'*What? We spend a fortune on sending you to an exclusive private school and you still say 'I's'.*'

779 '**M**um, I'm not going to school today.'

'*Why not?*'

'Because it's Sunday.'

780   **E**nglish teacher: *'Jamie, give me a sentence beginning with I'.*

Jamie: *'I is …'.*

Teacher: *'No Jamie, you must always say 'I am'.'*

Jamie: *'Okay. I am the ninth letter of the alphabet.'*

781   **E**nglish teacher: *'Spell Mississippi.'*

Student: *'The river or the state?'*

782   **G**eography teacher: *'What's the coldest country in the world?'*

Student: *'Chile.'*

You look so cold… you must surely be from Chile… or Alaska …or Siberia

No… I pack the frozen peas down at the local supermarket!'

783   **H**istory teacher: *'Here is a question to check that you did your homework on British kings and queens. Who came after Mary?'*

Student: *'Her little lamb.'*

784   **H**istory teacher: *'What was Camelot?'*

Student: *'A place where camels are parked.'*

785   **H**istory teacher: *'What's a Grecian Urn?'*

Student: *'About $500 a week.'*

786 History teacher: *'What's the best thing about history?'*

Mary: *'All the dates.'*

787 History teacher: *'Why do we refer to the period around 1000 years AD as the Dark Ages?'*

Student: *'Because there were so many knights.'*

788 Maths teacher: *'Paul. If you had five pieces of chocolate and Sam asked for one of them, how many would you have left?'*

Paul: *'Five.'*

789 Never go to school on an empty stomach. Go on the bus instead.

790 Principal: *'You should have been here at 9.00.'*

Student: *'Why, what happened?'*

791 In which class do you learn how to shop for bargains?

Buy-ology.

792 **S**cience teacher: *'What are nitrates?'*
Student: *'Cheaper than day rates.'*

793 **S**cience teacher: *'Which travels faster, heat or cold?'*
Student: *'Heat, because you can catch a cold.'*

794 **S**tudent to teacher: *'I don't want to worry you but my dad said that if my grades don't improve, someone's going to get a spanking.'*

795 **S**tudent: *'Would you punish someone for something they didn't do?'*
Teacher: *'Of course not.'*
Student: *'Good, because I didn't do my homework.'*

796 **W**hat's the difference between a train station and a teacher?
One minds the train, the other trains the mind.

797 **T**eacher: *'I wish you'd pay a little attention.'*

Student: *'I'm paying as little attention as possible.'*

798 **T**eacher: *'Wally, why are you late?'*

Wally: *'The train had a flat tire.'*

799 **T**eacher: *'That's three times I've asked you a question. Why won't you reply?'*

'Because you told me not to answer you back.'

Making Music

800 **M**usician 1: *'Who was that piccolo I saw you with last night?'*

Musician 2: *'That was no piccolo. That was my fife.'*

801 **'M**y singing teacher said I have voice made in heaven.'

'No she didn't. She said it was like nothing on earth.'

802 **W**hich Christmas song is popular in the Sahara Desert?

O Camel Ye Faithful.

803 **'O**ur Jackie learnt to play the violin in no time at all.'

'So I can hear.'

804 **W**hat do you call a guy who hangs around musicians?

A drummer.

805 **W**hat do you call a small Indian guitar?

A baby sitar.

806 **W**hat type of music do geologists like best?

Rock.

807 **W**hat was Pavarotti before he was a tenor?

A niner.

808 **W**here do musicians live?
In A flat.

The painful murder of the "1812 Overture"

809 **'T**his piece of music is haunting.'
'That's because you're murdering it.'

810 **H**ow do you make a bandstand?
Take away their chairs.

811 **'I** played Beethoven last night?'
'Who won?'

I wish someone would move me closer to the candles...so I could thaw out enough to blow them out!

812 **'W**hat shall I sing next.'
'Do you know 'Bridge Over Troubled Waters?''
'Yes.'
'Then go and jump off it.'

813 **W**hat do Eskimos sing at birthday parties?
'Freeze a Jolly Good Fellow.'

814 **W**hat's green and sings?

Elvis Parsley.

815 **W**hat does a musician take to the supermarket?

A Chopin Lizst.

816 **W**hat instrument does a fisherman play?

A cast-a-net.

817 **W**hy couldn't the composer be found?

Because he was Haydn.

818 **W**hy did the singer climb a ladder?

To reach the high notes.

819 **W**hy was the musician in prison?

Because he was always getting into treble.

Crossbreeds

820 **W**hat do you get when you cross a baby rabbit with a vegetable?

A bunion.

821 **W**hat do you get when you cross a black bird with a madman?

A raven lunatic.

822 **W**hat do you get when you cross a book with some perfume?

A best smeller.

823 **W**hat do you get when you cross a bear with a cow?

Winnie the Moo.

Gee! Thanks! What is it? Do I cuddle it ... or do I milk it?

824 What do you get when you cross a bridge with a car?

To the other side of the river.

825 What do you get when you cross a bushranger with a dessert?

Ned Jelly.

826 What do you get when you cross a chicken with a cement mixer?

A bricklayer.

827 What do you get when you cross a cow with a clairvoyant?

A message from the udder side.

828 What do you get when you cross a cow with a duck?

Cream quackers.

829 **W**hat do you get when you cross a shark with a crocodile with a Tyrannosauraus Rex?

I don't know, but don't take it swimming.

830 **W**hat do you get when you cross a cow with a whale?

Mooby dick.

831 **W**hat do you get when you cross a dinosaur with a computer?

A mega-bite.

832 **W**hat do you get when you cross a criminal with a rubbish collector?

Organised grime.

833 **W**hat do you get when you cross a doctor with a comedian?

A surgeon who has their patients in stitches.

834 **W**hat do you get when you cross a flower with a wally?

A blooming idiot.

835 **W**hat do you get when you cross a frog with a native American?

A toadempole.

836 **W**hat do you get when you cross a flea with a comedian?

A nitwit.

837 **W**hat do you get when you cross a flower with a big cat who wears a cravat?

A dandelion.

838 **W**hat do you get when you cross a hairdresser with a surfer?

Permanent waves.

839 **W**hat do you get when you cross a hare with a walking stick?

A hurry-cane (hurricane).

840 **W**hat do you get when you cross a heater with a witch?

A hot spell.

841 **W**hat do you get when you cross a hippopotamus with someone who is always sick?

A hippochondriac.

842 **W**hat do you get when you cross a jungle animal with an accountant?

A wild bore.

843 **W**hat do you get when you cross a kookaburra with a jug of gravy?

A laughing stock.

844 **W**hat do you get when you cross a master criminal with a fish?

The Codfather.

845 **W**hat do you get when you cross a kangaroo with a skyscraper?

A high jumper.

Is that the CODFATHER?

Yep...sure is! What a nasty piece of fish

846 **W**hat do you get when you cross a mouse and a deer?

Mickey Moose.

847 **W**hat do you get when you cross a mouse with an orange?

A pipsqueak.

848 **W**hat do you get when you cross a nun with a chicken?

A pecking order.

849 **W**hat do you get when you cross a parrot with a soldier?

A parrot trooper.

850 **W**hat do you get when you cross a painter with a police officer?

A brush with the law.

851 **W**hat do you get when you cross a plumber with a ballerina?

A tap dancer.

852 **W**hat do you get when you cross a police officer with a ghost?

An inspectre.

853 **W**hat do you get when you cross a seagull with a pair of wheels?

A bi-seagull.

854 **W**hat do you get when you cross a sheep with a radiator?

Central bleating.

855 **W**hat do you get when you cross a skunk with a table tennis ball?

Ping pong.

856 **W**hat do you get when you cross a wedding with a cliff?

A marriage that is on the rocks.

Their marriage was doomed from the start...he wanted a cliffside wedding... she didn't...

857 **W**hat do you get when you cross a snake with a builder?

A boa constructor.

858 **W**hat do you get when you cross a skunk with an owl?

A bird who stinks but doesn't give a hoot.

859 **W**hat do you get when you cross a snowman with a Cuban?

An ice cube.

860 **W**hat do you get when you cross a watch with a parrot?

Politicks.

Yuk! What stinks?

I don't know.... but I hope it's me!

861 **W**hat do you get when you cross a witch and a skunk?

An ugly smell.

862 **W**hat do you get when you cross a vampire with a computer?

Love at first byte.

863 **W**hat do you get when you cross an airplane with some pastry?

Pie in the sky.

Would Sir like peas with his pie...and perhaps a drink from our selection?

864 **W**hat do you get when you cross an Apple computer with fast food?

A Big Mac.

865 **W**hat do you get when you cross an overheating Apple computer with fast food?

A Big Mac and fries.

866 **W**hat do you get when you cross an elephant with a bottle of rum?

Trunk and disorderly.

Someone suggested a game of 'HERE COMES THE LION' at Jumbo's 3rd Birthday party startling his 2 ton friends into a stampede.

867 **W**hat do you get when you cross an elephant with a cake?

Crumbs.

868 **W**hat do you get when you cross an English king with a fireplace?

Alfred the Grate.

869 **W**hat do you get when you cross an elephant with a rhino?

Elifino.

Changing Light Bulbs

870 **H**ow many teachers does it take to change a light bulb?

None, they leave it to their students as an exercise.

871 **H**ow many accountants does it take to change a light bulb?

Sorry, there's no money left in the budget for another light bulb.

872 **H**ow many archaeologists does it take to change a light bulb?

Five, one to change it, the others to argue about the age of the old one.

873 **H**ow many actors does it take to change a light bulb?

Two, one to change it, the other to criticise his performance.

874 **H**ow many aerobic teachers does it take to change a light bulb?

Five, one to change it, the others to say, 'A Little to the left, a little to the right, a little to the left, a little to the right.'

875 **H**ow many astronomers does it take to change a light bulb?

None, they prefer the dark.

876 How many baseball players does it take to change a light bulb?

Two, one to change it, the other to signal which way to do it.

877 How many bureaucrats does it take to change a light bulb?

None, until the correct form has been filled out—in triplicate.

878 How many cave men does it take to change a light bulb?

What light bulbs?

879 How many cheapskates does it take to change a light bulb?

None, they'd prefer to sit in the dark.

880 How many circus performers does it take to change a light bulb?

Five, one to change it, the others to hold the net.

881 **H**ow many country music singers does it take to change a light bulb?

Two, one to change it, the other to sing about how heartbroken he is that the old one is finished.

882 **H**ow many clothing shop assistants does it take to change a light bulb?

Three, one to change it, one to say how well it fits and one to say that the colour is perfect.

883 **H**ow many elephants does it take to change a light bulb?

Two, but it has to be a pretty big light bulb!

884 **H**ow many hamsters does it take to change a light bulb?

Don't be silly, how would a hamster get up to a light bulb.

885 **H**ow many executives does it take to change a light bulb?

'First we have to hold a series of meetings to discuss the issue.'

886 **H**ow many fire officers does it take to change a light bulb?

Four, one to change it, the others to stand by with a hose.

887 **H**ow many fishermen does it take to change a light bulb?

Ten, one to change it, the others to argue about how big it is.

888 **H**ow many gardeners does it take to change a light bulb?

It depends whether it's the right season to change bulbs.

889 **H**ow many jugglers does it take to change a light bulb?

Just one, but they need three light bulbs.

There's always one in every crowd. Someone willing to try on the HEY Look trick in the middle of a juggling act.

890 **H**ow many kite fliers does it take to change a light bulb?

Ten, one to change it and the other nine to blow as hard as they can to get a wind going.

891 **H**ow many lawyers does it take to change a light bulb?

Three, one to sue the power company, one to sue the electrician who wired the house, and one to sue the bulb manufacturers.

892 **H**ow many magicians does it take to change a light bulb?

What do you want it changed into?

893 **H**ow many models does it take to change a light bulb?

None, they don't want to ruin their nails.

894 **H**ow many movie directors does it take to change a light bulb?

One, but he wants it done over and over again until he's perfectly happy.

895 **H**ow many punk rockers does it take to change a light bulb?

Two, one to change it and the other to smash the old one on his forehead.

896 **H**ow many optimists does it take to change a light bulb?

None, they reckon the power will come on without a bulb.

897 **H**ow many pessimists does it take to change a light bulb?

It doesn't matter, they reckon a new one will blow straight away anyway.

898 **H**ow many philosophers does it take to change a light bulb?

Well, that's a very interesting question.

899 **H**ow many politicians does it take to change a light bulb?

Three, one to change it, one to change it back, and a third to deny a change had ever taken place.

900 **H**ow many robots does it take to change a light bulb?

One, but it needs 500 humans to have programmed it correctly.

901 **H**ow many road workers does it take to change a light bulb?

Seven, one to change it, five to stand around leaning on their shovels and one to go and fetch lunch for them all.

902 **H**ow many roadies does it take to change a light bulb?

'One two, one two, one two.'

903 **H**ow many safety inspectors does it take to change a light bulb?

Ten, one to change it and the nine to hold the ladder.

904 **H**ow many siblings does it take to change a light bulb?

'It's your turn, I did it last time.' 'No you didn't, I did.' 'I did.' 'I did.'

905 **H**ow many skunks does it take to change a light bulb?

A phew.

I don't know how many soccer players it takes to change a lightbulb... but whoever kicked the ball can change it

906 **H**ow many soccer players does it take to change a light bulb?

Eleven, one to change it, the others to jump about, hugging and kissing him.

907 **H**ow many Santa Claus does it take to change a light bulb?

None, because there is no Santa Claus.

908 **H**ow many surgeons does it take to change a light bulb?

One, but only when a donor bulb is available.

You should have seen it Tracey! I'd been on the phone with Travis for 6 hours on Saturday when ...BANG off went the light! Dad had turned it off on me!

909 **H**ow many teenage girls does it take to change a light bulb?

One, but she'll be on the phone for five hours telling all her friends about it.

910 **H**ow many taxi drivers does it take to change a light bulb?

None, they won't even change a $5 note.

911 **H**ow many tourists does it take to change a light bulb?

Ten, one to take it and the other nine to take photos.

912 **H**ow many waiters does it take to change a light bulb?

None, not even a blown globe can catch a waiter's eye.

913 **O**ne.

How many psychics does it take to change a light bulb?

What a Wally

914 **'W**ally, what's the weather like.'

'I don't know. It's too foggy to tell.'

915 **A** wally went to the train station

Wally: *'I'd like a return ticket please?'*

Ticket seller: *'Certainly sir, where to?'*

'Back here of course.'

916 **D**id you hear about the wally firing squad?

They stood in a circle.

917 A wally was just about to dive into a pool when a lifesaver came rushing up.

Lifesaver: *'Don't jump. There's no water in the pool.'*

Wally: *'It's okay. I can't swim.'*

918 Did you hear about the wally burglar?

He robbed a music store and stole the lute.

919 Did you hear about the wally glass blower?

He inhaled and got a pane in the tummy.

920 Did you hear about the wally pirate?

He had a patch over both eyes.

921 **D**id you hear about the wally helicopter pilot?

He switched off the propeller because he couldn't stand the draft.

922 **D**id you hear about the wally school kid who was studying Greek Mythology?

When the teacher asked him to name something that was half-man and half-beast he replied 'Buffalo Bill.'

923 **D**id you hear about the wally secretary?

She was so good she could type sixty mistakes a minute?

924 **D**id you hear about the wally shoe repairman?

A customer gave him a pair of shoes to be soled, so he sold them.

925 **D**id you hear about the wally who had a brain transplant?

The brain rejected him.

926 **D**id you hear about the wally shoplifter?

He hurt his back trying to lift the corner store.

927 **D**id you hear about the other wally shoplifter?

He stole a free sample.

928 **D**id you hear about the wally terrorist who was told to blow up a car?

He burnt his mouth on the exhaust pipe.

929 **D**id you hear about the wally who locked his keys in the car?

He called a mechanic to get his family out.

930 **D**id you hear about the wally water polo player?

His horse drowned.

931 **D**id you hear about the wally who spent two hours in a department store?

He was looking for a cap with a peak at the back.

Boy! These caps with a peak at the back are hard to come by! But at last I found one.

932 **D**id you hear about the wally who stole a calendar?

He got twelve months.

933 **D**id you hear about the wally glazier who tried to fit a new window?

He broke it with a hammer.

934 **D**id you hear about the wally who saw a sign outside a bank saying 'Man Wanted for Bank Robbery'?

He went inside and applied for the job.

935 **D**id you hear about the wally who wanted value for money?

He sat at the back of the bus to get a longer ride.

936 **D**id you hear about the wally who went skiing?

He skied up the slope and caught the chair lift down.

937 **H**ow did the wally burn his ear?

He was ironing when the phone rang.

938 **D**id you hear about the wally who went water-skiing?

He spent his whole holiday looking for a sloping lake.

939 **H**ow do you get a one-armed wally out of a tree?

Wave to him.

940 **D**id you hear about the wally who went on a package tour near where the brain-eating headhunters live?

He was the only survivor.

941 **W**hat about the wally who burnt both his ears?

The caller rang back.

942 How do you compliment a wally?

Tell him he has an open mind.

943 How many wallies does it take to change a light bulb?

Five, one to climb the ladder, the others to turn the ladder around and around.

944 Three men were sentenced to death by firing squad. Just as they applied the blindfold to the first man, he yelled 'CYCLONE'. In the confusion, he escaped. Just as they applied the blindfold to the second man, he yelled 'FLOOD'. In the confusion, he escaped. The third man was a bit of a wally. Just as they applied the blindfold to him, he yelled out 'FIRE'.

945 What did the wally window cleaner have on the top of his ladder?

A stop sign.

946 Two wallies were walking home one night.

Wally 1: *'Is that the sun or the moon?'*

Wally 2: *'I don't know, I don't live around here.'*

Well there's not a lot of anything inside there!

RATTLE CLUNK

947 **W**hat do you call a flea who flies inside a wally's head?

A space invader.

948 **W**hat do you call a red-headed wally?

A ginger nut.

949 **W**hat do you call a wally with half a brain?

A genius.

950 **W**hat do wally kids do at Halloween?

They carve a face on an apple and go bobbing for pumpkins.

Bob's thick gravy was thicker than he was... but still he persisted for more than an hour to get it onto what was by then... COLD meat.

951 **W**hat does a wally pour over his meat?

Thick gravy.

952 **W**hy did the wally farmer pack up and move to the city?

Because he'd heard that the country was at war.

953 **W**hy did the wally get 17 of his friends to accompany him to the movies?

Because he'd heard it was not for under-18s.

954 **W**hy did the wally drive into the river?

He was trying to dip his headlights.

955 **W**hy did the wally put on a red coat and top hat and carry a telephone line under his arm?

He thought he had been invited to go fax hunting.

956 **W**hy did the wally quit his job as a telephonist?

Because he kept hearing voices.

957 **W**hy did the wally take a gun with him on his white-water rafting holiday?

So he could shoot the rapids.

958 **W**hy did the wally throw away his doughnut?

Because it had a hole in the middle.

959 **W**hy did the wally walk into the electricity company with a $20 note in each ear?

Because he'd received a bill saying he was $40 in arrears.

960 **W**hy do wally workers only get a half-hour lunch break?

Because if they took any longer, they would have to be re-trained.

961 **W**hy do wally's always have stupid grins on their face?

Because they're stupid.

962 **H**ow many toes does a wally have?

Take off your socks and count them.

963 **W**hy didn't the wally goalkeeper catch the ball?

He thought that's what the net was for.

Insults

964 You're so dumb, when your teacher said she wanted you to get ahead, she really meant 'a head'.

965 You're such a bad cook, even the maggots get take-away.

966 Your family is so poor, when the doorbell rings your sister has to shout out 'Ding, Dong.'

967 You're so dumb, when you went to the mind reader they couldn't find anything to read.

968 You're so slow, you can't even catch your breath.

969 As an outsider, what do you think of the human race?

970 Don't let your mind wander—it's too little to be let out alone.

971 Everyone has the right to be ugly, but you abused the privilege.

972 You are as useless as a screen door on a submarine.

973 With you here, your village must be missing its idiot.

974 You would be out of your depth in a puddle.

975 Here's 50 cents. Call all your friends and bring me back the change.

976 Your dog is so slow, he brings in last week's newspaper.

977 Turn the other cheek. On second thoughts, don't. The view is just as ugly on that side.

978 Is it true your brother is an only child?

979 You're not as stupid as you look. That would be impossible.

980 I'd leave you with one thought if you had somewhere to put it.

981 You're so dumb, it take you an hour to cook one-minute noodles.

982 You're so dumb, you think the English Channel is a British TV station.

983 You're so dumb, you took your mobile phone back to the shop because it came without a cord.

984 Your feet are so smelly, your shoes refuse to come out of the closet.

985 If someone offered you a penny for your thoughts, they'd expect some change.

986 You're so dumb, when you eat M&Ms, you throw out the Ws.

987 You have an open mind. Ideas just slip straight out.

988 You're so ugly, when you enter a room, the mice jump on chairs.

989 You're dark and handsome. When it's dark, you're handsome.

Has anyone ever told you how handsome you are with the lights OFF?

990 Last time I saw someone as ugly as you, I had to pay admission.

991 Instead of drinking from the fountain of knowledge, you just gargled.

992 If it's true that opposites attract, you'll meet someone who is good-looking, intelligent, and cultured.

993 They say that truth is stranger than fiction. And you're the proof.

994 **S**omeone told me you're not fit to live with pigs but I stuck up for you and said you were.

995 **I**'ll never forget the first time we met—although I keep trying.

996 **Y**ou're so dumb you stared at the orange juice container because it said 'Concentrate'.

997 **Y**ou're so dumb it takes you three hours to watch Sixty Minutes.

998 **Y**ou're so boring, you won't even talk to yourself.

999 **Y**ou're so ugly, the only dates you get are on a calendar.

1000 You're so ugly you have to trick or treat over the phone.

1001 You're growing on me—like a wart.